-ay as in clay

Mary Elizabeth Salzmann

Consulting Editor Monica Marx, M.A./Reading Specialist

Published by SandCastle™, an imprint of ABDO Publishing Company, 4940 Viking Drive, Edina, Minnesota 55435.

Printed in the United States.

Credits
Edited by: Pam Price
Curriculum Coordinator: Nancy Tuminelly
Cover and Interior Design and Production: Mighty Media
Photo Credits: Banana Stock Ltd., Brand X Pictures, Comstock, Corbis Images, Corel, Hemera, PhotoDisc, Stockbyte

Library of Congress Cataloging-in-Publication Data

Salzmann, Mary Elizabeth, 1968-
     -Ay as in clay / Mary Elizabeth Salzmann.
         p. cm. -- (Word families. Set VII)
     Summary: Introduces, in brief text and illustrations, the use of the letter combination "ay" in such words as "clay," "bay," "spray," and "tray."
     ISBN 1-59197-264-7
     1. Readers (Primary) [1. Vocabulary. 2. Reading.] I. Title. II. Series.

PE1119 .S2342149 2003
428.1--dc21   2002038217

SandCastle™ books are created by a professional team of educators, reading specialists, and content developers around five essential components that include phonemic awareness, phonics, vocabulary, text comprehension, and fluency. All books are written, reviewed, and leveled for guided reading, early intervention reading, and Accelerated Reader® programs and designed for use in shared, guided, and independent reading and writing activities to support a balanced approach to literacy instruction.

Let Us Know

After reading the book, SandCastle would like you to tell us your stories about reading. What is your favorite page? Was there something hard that you needed help with? Share the ups and downs of learning to read. We want to hear from you! To get posted on the ABDO Publishing Company Web site, send us e-mail at:

sandcastle@abdopub.com

SandCastle Level: Transitional

-ay Words

clay

gray

hay

jay

spray

tray

Don plays with blue
and yellow clay.

Jane sits on a gray wall.

The kitten sits on a bale of hay.

The mother jay feeds
the babies.

Ed has fun in the spray.

Nan carries her lunch on a tray.

Ray Visits May for a Day

Ray went to spend the day
with his friend May McKay.

May lives on a farm
not too far away.

Ray met May's parents
and her big brother, Clay.

They went to the barn, and
on the roof was a blue jay.

May showed Ray
her donkey, and it
gave a loud bray.

Next she showed Ray
her pig named Fay.

Ray helped feed the
chickens, who lay eggs
every day.

Ray learned that May's horse is a bay.

Then Ray and May
climbed on bales of hay.

At lunchtime, Mrs. McKay
brought their food
on a tray.

Then she turned on the
sprinkler so they could play
in the spray.

Ray had so much fun that
he wished he could stay.

The -ay Word Family

bay	lay
bray	May
clay	McKay
day	play
Fay	Ray
gray	spray
hay	stay
jay	tray

Glossary

Some of the words in this list may have more
than one meaning. The meaning listed here
reflects the way the word is used in the book.

bale   a bundle of hay or straw
tied tightly together

bay   a horse with a reddish
brown body and a black
mane and tail

bray   the loud, harsh noise
made by a donkey

donkey   an animal that's related to
the horse, but is smaller
with longer ears

jay   a bird with a white body
and black and blue wings

sprinkler   a device that sprays water
over a yard or garden

About SandCastle™

A professional team of educators, reading specialists, and content developers created the SandCastle™ series to support young readers as they develop reading skills and strategies and increase their general knowledge. The SandCastle™ series has four levels that correspond to early literacy development in young children. The levels are provided to help teachers and parents select the appropriate books for young readers.

Emerging Readers
(no flags)

Beginning Readers
(1 flag)

Transitional Readers
(2 flags)

Fluent Readers
(3 flags)

These levels are meant only as a guide. All levels are subject to change.

To see a complete list of SandCastle™ books and other nonfiction titles from ABDO Publishing Company, visit **www.abdopub.com** or contact us at:

4940 Viking Drive, Edina, Minnesota 55435 • 1-800-800-1312 • fax: 1-952-831-1632